Design Your Dream Home

Interior Decorating and Design Tips

Table of Contents

Chapter 1. Introduction

Welcome to your dream let's-turn-this-house-into-a-home journey! Our special report on "Design Your Dream Home: Interior Decorating and Design Tips" is a vibrant, image-filled guide that will not only inspire your creative decoration ideas but also include practical advice to help you transform your living space into your personal paradise. This report breaks the process down into simple, achievable steps that'll have you brimming with excitement and anticipation, assuring your confidence to purchase it. So, come on over, dive in and let your home decor dreams turn into a blissful, tangible reality! Happy decorating!

Chapter 2. Understanding Your Space and Style

Before jumping into the world of interior design and decoration, it's vital to have a comprehensive understanding of your space and personal style. This chapter will guide you in determining what you like, what you need, and how you can make the most out of your space.

Let's start with the basics.

2.1. Understanding Your Space

When evaluating your space, there are several aspects to consider.

One of the initial steps of interior design is knowing the floor plan. Observe and take notes of your space in its raw form. Map out your area, be it a single room or an entire house. Measure the length, breadth, and height of each room, and jot down these details. Measurements are critical for planning the furniture layout and ensuring that everything fits perfectly.

Next, consider the architectural style of your house. Is it modern, traditional, Victorian, or perhaps mid-century? The architectural style can influence your interior design decisions, ensuring there's a harmonious connection between the structure and your decorative elements.

Don't forget the importance of natural light. Note down which rooms get the most sunlight, and at what time of the day. Sunlight can dramatically affect the mood and visual appeal of a room. Its abundance can make a room feel more open and friendly, while a lack of sunlight might call for careful artificial lighting design.

2.1.1. Traffic Flow

In any home, there are certain patterns of movement, this is called traffic flow. Take time to notice how you and others move around the house. Identify any congested areas that could benefit from a better layout or obstacles that can be eliminated. A well-considered traffic flow can significantly improve the functionality and comfort of your home.

All these elements (measurements, architectural style, sunlight, traffic flow) contribute significantly to understanding your space. Keep these parameters in mind as you envision your design concept.

2.2. Discovering Your Style

While understanding your space is essential, it's equally important to know your style. Your home should reflect who you are. There are many interior design styles, so don't be surprised or overwhelmed if you find yourself drawn to more than one.

Here's a basic guide to common interior design styles:

1. Modern: Characterized by simplicity, functionality, and clean lines.

2. Traditional: Features classic details, sumptuous furnishings, and an abundance of accessories.

3. Rustic: Emphasizes rugged, natural beauty, incorporating raw and often unfinished elements.

4. Bohemian: Reflects a carefree, relaxed, and unique aesthetic.

Identify what aspects you like from each style, this can help you create a more personalized "eclectic" style.

As you explore these styles, also consider your color preferences. Colors play a critical role in conveying style and atmosphere. From calming blues and greens to energizing yellows and reds, your color choices will have a significant psychological impact on the inhabitants.

Furthermore, think about textures and patterns. Velvet, silk, wool, linen, cotton each has its own appeal. Similarly, patterns like stripes, floral, or geometric designs can help express your unique taste.

2.3. Integrate Your Lifestyle

When designing your space, it must not only look good but also align with your lifestyle. If you often host dinner parties, a larger dining area with comfortable seating might be beneficial. If you work from home, a quiet workspace with a suitable desk and ergonomic chair is essential. So, reflect on your daily activities and let them guide your design choices.

2.4. Putting It Together

After evaluating your space and determining your style, it's time to merge these two components. Take your measurements, architectural details, sunlight, traffic flow, and interior design styles, and begin imagining how all these factors will come together.

Remember, your home is an extension of your personality; it should not just be trendy but reflect your personal taste. So, be patient, take your time, and enjoy the process of creating a home that truly feels like 'you'.

Chapter 3. Color Schemes: Harmony and Contrast

Color balancing is where the magic truly begins in home decor. The color scheme you decide on will create the mood for your entire space, establishing harmony, delivering contrast, or creating a unique blend of both. The choice of colors can make a small room appear spacious, a large one cozier, or even influence the perception of room height. The art of managing colors with taste and judgment involves understanding the basic principles of color theory and applying them to match the purpose and aesthetic of your space.

Let's delve into the fascinating world of color schemes, exploring the essential elements of color harmony and contrast, and how they can interplay to create an unforgettable ambiance.

3.1. Understanding Color Theory

At the heart of achieving visual harmony lies the science and art of color theory. A comprehension of color theory involves understanding, among other elements, the color wheel. Built on the primary colors—red, yellow, and blue—and their combinations, it is your guide to figuring out what colors work well together.

Color relationships are the foundation of color harmony. Three vital color relationships are:

1. Complementary colors - Colors straight across from each other on the color wheel (e.g., red and green, or blue and orange).

2. Analogous colors - Colors situated next to each other on the color wheel (e.g., yellow, yellow-green, and green).

3. Triadic colors - Three colors equally spaced around the color wheel (e.g., primary colors: red, yellow, and blue).

Choosing colors within these relationships sets the groundwork for an aesthetically pleasing palette.

3.2. Choosing a Color Scheme: Base, Accent, and Neutral Colors

When faced with the abundance of color choices, it can be challenging to decide where to start. A widely accepted approach involves picking three different types of colors - base, accent, and neutral.

The base color is usually the dominant color and sets the overall tone of the room. Commonly applied to walls, it serves as the backdrop to your creative canvas. Accent colors, on the other hand, are vibrant and used sparingly. They can be introduced through accessories like cushions, rugs, or artwork to add an element of surprise or energy. Neutral colors help balance everything out. They give the eyes a place to rest amidst the interaction of base and accent colors.

3.3. Color Harmony: Building an Eye-Pleasing Color Palette

A harmonious color palette is a key player in establishing the mood of a room - calming, energizing, or anything in between. The objective here is to create an agreeable interaction of colors that provides visual ease and comfort. Depending on the intended ambiance, this might involve sticking to analogous colors, using different shades of a single color, or opting for a monochromatic scheme.

Remember, color harmony isn't just about colors that go well together. It's more about the overall effect they build together. It should reflect your taste, complement your lifestyle, and enhance your living space.

3.4. Color Contrast: Adding Interest and Spark

While color harmony aims to create a visual serenity, color contrast, on the other hand, is all about creating visual interest and catchiness. The use of contrasting colors gives depth and dimension to a room. It draws the eye and can highlight important design elements.

Contrast isn't confined to color alone. You can play with variations in texture, shape, and size as well. A smooth, neutral-colored leather couch against a rustic, brick red wall, or a sleek metal table paired with a fluffy, white rug. These juxtapositions add layers to your decor, enhancing its visual impact.

3.5. Using Color to Influence Perception of Space

Colors don't just affect the mood, they can also trick the eye and alter the perception of space. Bright, light colors like whites, creams, or pastels can make a small room seem bigger and brighter by reflecting more light. Dark, rich colors bring warmth and intimacy, best suited for larger rooms to make them feel cozier.

3.6. Lighting's Impact on Color

Color does not stay constant and shifts depending on the intensity and type of light. Natural daylight shows the truest color, while incandescent lighting brings out warm tones and yellows. Fluorescent lighting casts a sharp blue tone. Avoid color mishaps by testing your paint or color swatches under different lighting conditions.

3.7. Conclusion: Letting Intuition Guide You

Color psychology and theory offer guiding principles in picking a color scheme. However, at the end of the day, your home is a unique expression of you. Let your intuition guide your color decisions, creating a space that feels just right for you.

Whether looking to achieve serene harmony or stark contrast, understanding how colors interact and influence space is key. Your color scheme is essentially your canvas. A well-placed stroke of color can make your home more welcoming, create dramatic interest, or even set the mood for a comforting retreat.

Remember, home decor is an ongoing journey of discovery and expression. So, feel free to experiment with your color schemes, altering them with changing moods, seasons, or simply on a whim.

Chapter 4. Smart Furniture Selection: Comfort and Aesthetics

Choosing the right furniture for your home is an essential task to balance both comfort and aesthetics. The process can either be a delightful journey of creativity or a grueling endeavor that leaves you confused and exhausted. However, with a synergy of smart strategy, insightful planning, suitable budgeting, and leaning on your unique style, furniture selection can indeed be a rewarding endeavor. This chapter will guide you through this, breaking down the process into digestible chunks.

4.1. Understand Your Space

Before you run to the nearest furniture store, take a moment to understand your space. Ideas might be overflowing, but without knowing the dimensions, you can't make a realistic choice. While dealing with space, consider the following:

1. Size: Measure the room dimensions to understand what size of furniture can fit correctly without making the space look cramped.

2. Layout: A space can have an open, closed, or semi-open layout, affecting the furniture placement.

3. Functionality: Your living room might double as a home office or your dining area as a kids' study area. Choose furniture that augments the room's functionality.

4. Existing elements: Built-in features like fireplaces, window views, built-in shelves or cabinets, or high ceilings can influence your choice of furniture.

4.2. Identify Your Style

There is a certain joy in identifying and owning your unique interior design style. It might be contemporary, traditional, rustic or even a blend of styles – a reflection of your personality. When selecting furniture, your style is your north star, guiding your selections and ensuring consistency. Find inspiration in various sources like design magazines, blogs, Instagram profiles of interior decorators, or even in the nooks and corners of your local cafes and friends' houses.

4.3. Budget Planning

Budgeting is a delicate part of the furniture selection process. To avoid a financial roller coaster ride, plan your budget wisely. Divide your budget into components, allocating a percentage for larger items like sofa and bed, and the rest for smaller elements like side tables, decorative items, etc. Remember, quality is not always synonymous with a hefty price tag. It's perfectly plausible to find durable and aesthetically pleasing furniture at mid-range and even budget prices.

4.4. Comfort Is Key

Comfort should never be compromised while selecting furniture. No matter how stylish a piece of furniture is, if it isn't comfortable, it will lose its value over time. Pay special attention to the comfort factor when choosing furniture pieces you'll use extensively, such as your bed, sofa, and office chair.

4.5. Furniture Materials and Finishes

Quality furniture starts with quality materials. Both the exterior finish and the interior structure matter in determining how long your furniture will last and how it will age. In addition to quality, the material and finish can also dictate the aesthetics of the room. For example, a leather sofa adds a certain level of elegance to a room, while a fabric one adds warmth.

4.6. Proportions and Scale

An important part of creating a well-balanced room is understanding the concept of scale and proportions. Furniture sizes should not only be based on room dimensions but also on the dimensions of other furniture and elements in the room.

4.7. Color and Texture

Colors speak volumes about a space. A calm, neutral palette might whisper of sophistication, while a bright, eclectic mix might shout out creativity. Textures can be equally exciting – they can soften, harden, cozy-up, or business-like a space often, on a subconscious level.

4.8. A Sustainable Approach

Sustainability is not just a social responsibility, but it also adds a sense of mindfulness to your interiors. You can incorporate sustainability in your furniture selection by choosing eco-friendly materials, opting for local artisans and manufacturers, and investing in durable furniture that won't need replacement shortly, hence reducing waste.

4.9. Custom versus Ready-made

You may have thought about whether to go for ready-made furniture or have it custom-built for you. Both have their merits, so consider each carefully before deciding.

Choosing furniture demands time and patience. But the rewards are indeed enticing – a comfortable, functional, and aesthetically pleasing space.

4.10. Shopping Smart

Know where to shop. Some stores specialize in certain lifestyles, designs, or categories. Recognize when it's worth splurging on a high-end piece or when you might find a deal at low-cost alternatives or even secondhand shops. Don't forget to test furniture in person whenever possible.

The road of furniture selection might seem winding and often baffling. However, with this guide, you are now armed with a roadmap to traverse this journey smoothly, creating a blissful harmony of comfort and aesthetics in your interiors. Enjoy the journey!

Chapter 5. Lighting Essentials: The Magic of Ambient, Task, and Accent

Lighting, often considered the unsung hero of interior design, plays a more significant role than merely illuminating a space. It creates ambiance, establishes mood, and can utterly transform even the most basic rooms into a cozy, luxurious haven. This chapter highlights how to utilize and balance the three types of lighting – ambient, task, and accent – to breathe life into your dream home.

5.1. The Basics of Lighting

Lighting design encompasses more than picking out stylish lamps or fixtures. It involves understanding how to use light effectively to both serve practical needs and create decorative effects. We categorize lighting into three central types: ambient, task, and accent. Ambient lighting offers overall illumination, task lighting aids in completing specific activities, and accent lighting adds drama and highlights focal points.

5.2. Ambient Lighting: The Foundation

Ambient lighting, also known as general lighting, provides overall illumination to a space and is the cornerstone of a good lighting plan. It ensures an even distribution of light across the room without heavy contrasts between light and dark. Ceiling-mounted or recessed fixtures that direct light downwards, wall sconces, or floor lamps are common sources of ambient lighting.

The key factor in ambient lighting is the understanding of natural light. Bear in mind the direction of your windows and the quality of light they allow through at various times of the day. Harness and augment this natural light effectively, then consider where additional sources are needed when daylight fades.

5.3. Task Lighting: Enhancing Functionality

Task lighting, as the name suggests, is used to support specific tasks like reading, cooking, studying, or applying makeup. It is geared towards functionality and should be adjustable and bright enough without casting shadows. Desk, table, and buffet lamps, along with pendant and track lights, under-cabinet lights in the kitchen, and vanity lights in the bathroom, fall into this category.

Implementing task lighting involves recognizing the parts of your home where tasks occur. Assess your space vigilantly – a corner nook may seem perfectly bright with ambient light during the day, but what about a cloudy afternoon or evening?

5.4. Accent Lighting: Bringing Drama

Accent lighting is primarily decorative. Its purpose is to draw the eye to specific areas or objects in a room, like artwork, architectural details, or bookcases. This form of lighting typically requires at least three times as much light on the focal point as the general lighting around it. Recessed or track lighting, wall-mounted picture lights, and uplights are typical sources of accent lighting.

Consider areas in your home that you'd like to highlight. That could be a prized painting, an architectural feature, or a uniquely textured wall. Accent lighting will let these features shine and turn them into captivating focal points.

5.5. Layering The Light

A well-lit room will have a balance of all three types of light. Layering the lights allows you to control the ambience and functionality of a space depending on the time of day, occasion, or your mood. You can create a dramatic effect by layering and combining different light sources at different levels to create a flattering ambience.

Select light fixtures of different heights to add depth to your rooms. Overhead lights, table lamps, floor lamps, and wall sconces can all work together to create different moods. For instance, in your living room, an overhead chandelier (ambient light) can work in harmony with a side table lamp near the reading nook (task light) and accent lights around a mantelpiece or showcasing art.

5.6. Choosing The Right Light Bulb

Remember, the kind of light bulb you use can significantly impact your space's overall ambiance. LED bulbs are energy-efficient and long-lasting, while incandescent bulbs provide a warm, inviting light. Be aware of the color temperature of bulbs, measured in Kelvins. A lower Kelvin number will produce a warm, cozy light, while a higher Kelvin number results in a cooler, more energizing light.

5.7. Conclusion

The unrivaled power of lighting is indeed fascinating. With a rich blend of ambient, task, and accent lighting, you can transform your home into your personal paradise, regardless of its size or architectural design. Lighting not only serves the fundamental purpose of visibility, but it also contributes to creating a welcoming atmosphere, enhancing colors and textures, and showcasing your unique style. By following these tips, you can illuminate your home so beautifully and effectively that it will truly feel like your dream come true.

Chapter 6. Textures and Patterns: The Secret Sauce of Interior Design

Understanding and incorporating varied textures and patterns in your home interior design can play a substantial role in creating an aesthetically pleasing and comfortable living space. This chapter will guide you through the significance of different textures and patterns while also giving you practical tips and creative ideas to enrich your decor.

6.1. Understanding Textures

In interior design, 'texture' refers to the surface quality of a material. Every surface has a texture, be it smooth or rough, soft or hard. Textures do not merely inform you about the physical feel of an object; it also contributes to the overall aesthetics of the room.

To appreciate the importance of texture in interior design, close your eyes and think about a room featuring only smooth textures. The sofa, the walls, the carpet, the curtains – everything is perfectly sleek and streamlined. While this might seem like a minimalist's dream, it could feel cold, stark, or impersonal.

Now, imagine a room filled with varied textures – a soft cashmere throw on a plush velvet sofa, a sleek marble coffee table on a fluffy shag rug, rustic wooden beams against a smooth painted wall. This room, in contrast, feels warm, inviting, and visually interesting.

Textures add depth and dimension to a room, making it more visually appealing. It isn't just about tactile experiences; visual textures play an essential role in home interior design. In many ways, texture is the secret ingredient that gives a room its character and transforms it from merely 'functional' to 'inviting'.

6.2. Incorporating Textures in Your Decor

Textiles are the easiest and most flexible way to add texture. Think of soft rugs underfoot or the feeling of slipping into a bed covered with smooth, fresh linen. Cushions in various materials, such as silk, wool, velvet or cotton, can dramatically alter the feel of your sofa. Likewise, window treatments also offer ample opportunities for incorporating diverse textures.

Furniture is another crucial element for textures. A leather sofa evokes a completely different feel compared to a cotton couch. The rough, grainy surface of a wooden coffee table stands in contrast to the cool smoothness of a glass top table.

Even walls and ceilings can join the texture party. Choose paint with a sandy texture for a subtle effect, or go bold with decorative plaster or exposed brick. Wallpaper, too, offers vast options for introducing colorful texture, from classic embossed designs to modern 3D patterns.

Accessories and ornaments which include baskets, vases, mirrors, artwork, and lamps also contribute to the texture story. The key is to mix and match, ensuring no surface or object feels too similar.

6.3. Understanding Patterns

Patterns are combinations or replications of multiple elements that create visual interest. They could be simple geometric shapes, intricate floral prints, abstract designs, or anything in between. Patterns add life and personality to your rooms, making them vibrant and interesting.

However, using patterns requires a delicate balance. Too much pattern can overwhelm the eye and make a space feel chaotic. Too little pattern can make a room feel dull and lifeless. Just the right amount of pattern, juxtaposed against solid colors, can add rhythm and interest to your home interior design.

6.4. Applying Patterns in Your Decor

Patterns can be added to your interior decor in a myriad of ways. Wallpaper and textiles are the most obvious choices. Wallpaper can create a feature wall with bold patterns or add a subtle backdrop with delicate designs. Similarly, patterned curtains, rugs, cushions, and upholstery can inject color and character into a room.

Pay attention to the scale and density of patterns. Large patterns work best on large surfaces, like walls and floors, or sizeable pieces of furniture. Small patterns are better suited to smaller areas or pieces.

Maintaining a balance is critical when mixing patterns. Aim for a harmony of scaled patterns, colors, and neutral breaks. Remember to space out patterns and provide areas of solid color to rest the eye.

Whether you choose to incorporate textures or patterns, they can indeed work wonders when executed with thought and precision. Understand them in depth, experiment with courage, and achieve a harmonious blend. It may take time to master, but the results will undoubtedly be worthwhile, illuminating your home with a unique aesthetics and personality.

6.5. Final Thoughts on Textures and Patterns

Textures and patterns are secret sauces of interior design. Though often overlooked in the process, they are what give a room its soul and energy. Strategic application and smart integration of different textures and patterns can alter and enhance the mood, depth, and visual weight of the rooms.

Remember that rules are just guidelines. Feel free to break them, take risks and make the space your own. After all, it's the personal touches and distinct style that make your house a home. So, go ahead and infuse these magic ingredients in your decor recipe, and witness your home bloom with warmth and beauty.

Chapter 7. Embracing Minimalism: Less is More

Throughout the evolution of interior design, numerous styles have emerged, each with its own charm and unique aesthetics. However, one particular approach that has had a significant impact in recent times is minimalism. With its roots in Japanese Zen philosophy and its focus on simplifying and decluttering, minimalism has found its place in many homes around the world, transforming them from cluttered, chaotic spaces into serene, streamlined interiors.

7.1. The Ideology of Minimalism

Before delving into the how-to's of minimalist design, it's important to understand the underlying ideology that makes this style what it is. Minimalism, in simple terms, is a design style that emphasizes the concept of "less is more". It's about stripping down to the essentials, eliminating unnecessary elements, and focusing on functionality without compromising aesthetics. The philosophy goes deeper than just a design style—it's a way of life. It's about living with less and finding pleasure in simplicity, believing that removing excess can lead to a calmer, happier, and more fulfilling lifestyle.

7.2. Benefits of Embracing Minimalism

When applied to your home, minimalism can be highly beneficial. Some of its advantages include the following:

1. A space that feels bigger: By eliminating clutter and embracing open space, you can create the illusion of a larger room. This makes minimalist design ideal for small apartments or houses.

2. A calming environment: A minimalistic room tends to be peaceful and calming. The lack of clutter and visual noise leads to a less stressful and more relaxed living environment.

3. Easier to clean: With fewer elements in a room, cleaning becomes a lot easier and quicker.

4. Highlights quality: Because minimalist spaces have fewer items, those that remain are the best and most loved.

7.3. Key Elements of Minimalist Interior Design

When it comes to decorating your home with a minimalist mindset, there are certain key elements that you should keep in mind. They include clarity, simplicity, functionality, and neutrality.

1. Clarity: Everything in a minimalist room has a purpose. Each piece of furniture, accessory, or artwork should contribute to the overall functionality and aesthetic of the space.

2. Simplicity: Avoid complex patterns, excessive decorations, and clutter. Keep things as simple and clean as possible.

3. Functionality: Every item in a minimalist home must serve a purpose. If it doesn't, it's considered clutter.

4. Neutrality: Neutral shades like white, beige, and gray often dominate minimalist interiors. These colors contribute to the serene, calm atmosphere that is characteristic of the style.

7.4. Incorporating Minimalism into Your Home

Embracing minimalism in your home doesn't mean completely renovating your living space or getting rid of everything you own. It's a matter of making thoughtful decisions and being comfortable with simplicity and clear space. Below are some steps to guide you.

7.4.1. Purge and Declutter

The very first step is decluttering. Evaluate your possessions and get rid of things you no longer use or need. Ask yourself: does this item serve a purpose? Does it bring me joy? Your answers will help you decide what to keep and what to part with.

7.4.2. Choose a Neutral Palette

A largely neutral palette is a defining characteristic of minimalist design. Think Tones of white, cream, beige, grey and pale pastels. They can create a calming, tranquil atmosphere in your home.

7.4.3. Functional and Essential Furniture

Every piece of furniture should be functional and chosen for a purpose and place. Avoid excessive or oversized furniture - the fewer pieces, the better.

7.4.4. Keep Surfaces Clear

Aim to keep as many surfaces as possible clear of items. This adds to the overall sense of calm and order. When necessary, use hidden storage solutions.

7.4.5. Selecting Decor Thoughtfully

When it comes to selecting decor, opt for fewer and more meaningful pieces. These could be art pieces, family photos, or plants.

Embracing minimalism doesn't necessarily mean you have to sacrifice comfort or personal style. It's about finding balance, discarding excess, and focusing on what brings utility and joy to your life. The less you have, the more you appreciate what's left.

Chapter 8. Eclectic Style: Mixing Old and New

Before we delve into the heart of eclectic style, it's crucial to understand that while it represents a vibrant mix of eras, cultures, and designs, it isn't about tossing everything into a pot and hoping it matches. Instead, it's about thoughtfully layering elements to create a space that's genuinely unique to your style preferences, marrying tradition with innovation, old with new.

8.1. Understanding Eclectic Style

Eclectic style embraces the harmony that can be found amidst contrasting pieces. It's the perfect platform for displaying a varied collection of furniture, artwork, fabrics, and accessories from different periods and styles. It's an aesthetic that appeals to people who aren't interested in adhering to one particular style; those who love to mix and blend, creating truly unique spaces while ensuring a smooth visual flow.

The core philosophy behind eclectic style is the principle of unifying different design elements by using color, texture, and pattern. By layering these different elements cohesively, you can create rooms bursting with personality and interest.

8.2. Characteristics of Eclectic Style

While there isn't a steadfast manual for eclectic design due to its very nature, there are recurrent characteristics commonly seen in this style.

- **Balance and Scale:** The artful arrangement of mismatched items ensures they live harmoniously within the same space. A keen understanding of balance and scale is necessary to maintain unity.

- **Color Cohesion:** A recurrent color throughout the room can unify the different design elements. This trait applies to wall and furniture color or upholstery fabric, binding disparate pieces together.

- **Rich in Texture and Pattern:** Leather, linen, silk, velvet, wood, metal, and glass might all be present in an eclectic room. Similar can be said about patterns drawing from various cultures and eras.

- **Artistic Flair:** Artwork often serves as the focal point in an eclectic style home. The art itself can be a mishmash of styles and periods, emphasizing the room's overall design diversity.

8.3. Mixing Old and New

To create a successful eclectic look, it's essential to skillfully blend old and new elements. A common strategy is to add modern objects into a mostly traditional setting or vice versa. Here are a few tips on how to do this:

1. **Vintage with Modern:** Invigorate your space by harmonizing modern and vintage pieces. For instance, a sleek modern sofa blended with a vintage armchair — or even a traditional chandelier in an otherwise contemporary room — can spawn a fascinating eclectic style.

2. **Travel and Culture:** Merge items from your travels, like a tribal rug from Morocco and wooden sculptures from Bali, with a contemporary leather sofa or glass coffee table.

3. **Eras:** Mix furniture from different periods such as Mid-Century Modern accents in an industrial loft or Victorian lighting fixtures in a modern apartment.

The idea behind mixing old and new isn't just about the physical age of items but the periods, styles, and cultural associations they represent. Daring contrasts can infuse your space with an eclectic vibe.

8.4. Color in Eclectic Style

Color plays a massive role in unifying your eclectic ensemble. Opt for a complementary color scheme, like a mix of warm reds, oranges, and yellows, or cool blues, greens, and purples. Additionally, a neutral background might be ideal if your furniture and accessories are filled with color, helping highlight the brilliance of your eclectic collection.

8.5. Picking The Right Furniture

Selecting pieces that balance each other out is vital in eclectic decor. A bulky, vintage sofa can be seamlessly blended with a sleek, modern coffee table. With smart choices, these dissimilar pieces can complement each other in surprising ways. When picking furniture, be adventurous; find pieces you love, even if they're not of the same style.

8.6. Conclusion

Mastering the eclectic style is all about attaining harmony within diversity. Daring to mix instead of match, celebrating contrasts, and merging horizons create an incredibly personal, storytelling interior that reflects your unique character. Remember, use color, texture, and pattern to unite your various pieces, and most importantly, have fun with it. It's YOUR space, and it should reflect your personality, taste, and the many roles you play in life. After all, isn't that the allure of eclectic style?

Chapter 9. Creating a Theme: The Rooms That Tell Stories

Choosing a theme for your interior design isn't just about picking a palette or aesthetic that appeals to you. Instead, it's about creating rooms that tell stories - your stories - that say something about who you are and where you want to be.

9.1. The Importance of Themes

Creating a theme is, indeed, the starting point of your interior design journey. It's much like building the foundations for a house. Without a good foundational theme, the design appears disorganized, disjointed, or even chaotic.

Additionally, having a cohesive theme can optimize your decorating results. It streamlines your choices, determining the direction for them, and saves you from becoming overwhelmed by the numerous options available. Not only does a theme bring coherence to the decor, but it also adds a unique personality to your home - making it an extension of yourself.

9.2. Selecting a Theme: Points to Ponder

There is no 'one-size-fits-all' approach when it comes to choosing themes. Here are a few factors you need to contemplate:

- **Your Personal Style**: Determine what resonates with you personally. Do you relish in the elegance of classic designs, or do you cherish the simplicity and functionality of modern designs? Are you attracted to rustic elements, or do you prefer sleek, contemporary styles?

- **Lifestyle Considerations**: Your living conditions should be considered before choosing a theme. Think about your day-to-day activities, the number of people in the house, toddlers or pets, if any, and pick a theme that complements these factors.

- **Location of the House**: Also, factor in the architectural style and geographical location of your home. Beach houses may benefit from coastal themes, while an apartment in the city might be more suited to a modern industrial look.

9.3. Crafting Your Theme: Steps to Follow

Once you have a better idea regarding these factors, here is a step-by-step guide to help you formalize your theme:

- **Draw inspiration**: Look for ideas in home decor magazines, online platforms, television shows, and even arts, travel, or nature. Building an inspiration board - physical or digital - can be a great start.

- **Analyze the mood**: Understand and define the kind of mood you want to invite into your space. Do you want a peaceful, serene environment, or a vibrant, energy-filled room? This understanding will guide your selection of themes.

- **Create a color scheme**: With the mood in mind, develop a color scheme. Professionals recommend a 60-30-10 rule. 60% represents the dominant color, 30% is the secondary color, and the final 10% is for accent color(s).

- **Choose your furniture**: Furniture plays a crucial role in defining the theme of your room. Whether it's chic modern furniture for your minimalist theme or rich textures and antique pieces for a vintage theme, pick them carefully.

- **Detailing with decor**: Small details can make a huge difference. Decorative pieces, lighting, rugs, curtains, all these are ingredients that turn your theme into a tangible reality.

9.4. Changing Themes Across Rooms

A common question for many aspiring decorators is whether the theme should be consistent throughout the home. In general, it can lead to a cohesive sense of storytelling. However, it's completely acceptable to vary the themes room to room based on the specific purpose and feeling associated with each space.

Take your time to decide what theme each room should feature, what story it should tell. Remember, the most important consideration is that the theme should reflect your personal style and taste.

9.5. Conclusion

Theming your home doesn't necessarily entail sticking to stringent design rules. In fact, the best theme would be one that is truly authentic to you and your lifestyle. The ultimate objective of home decor is to rejuvenate and comfort you; hence, let your personal desires and needs lead the design process.

Creating a space that tells a story can seem challenging, but it becomes exponentially easier and more enjoyable when you phrase it as telling your story. Embrace this fascinating journey of self-expression and creativity and let your home become your canvas!

Chapter 10. Sustainable Designs: Eco-friendly and Stylish

Creating an eco-friendly, stylish environment in your home not only boosts your quality of life but also contributes positively to the planet. Here we cover simple yet innovative strategies to incorporate sustainability into your home, from energy-efficient appliances and solar panels to natural materials and biophilic designs. We also discuss the essence of sustainability — reducing, reusing, and recycling, key principles for eco-friendly home design.

10.1. Understanding Sustainability in Home Design

Sustainability is not just a trend, it's a lifestyle change that involves designing spaces with minimal environmental impact. This encompasses efficient use of resources, responsible sourcing of materials, and a lower carbon footprint. Sustainable design is a synergy of aesthetic appeal and environmental consciousness, enhancing your living experience while ensuring future generations will have a healthy world to live in.

Take a holistic approach to sustainable design; it should not just be about individual elements but also the overall flow and functionality of the space. Strive for harmony between aesthetics, functionality, and green vision.

10.2. Consider Eco-friendly Materials

Focus on responsibly sourced, sustainable materials. Opt for organic, renewable, or recycled materials whenever possible.

- Bamboo: This fast-growing, renewable resource can be transformed into framing materials, flooring, and furniture. Bamboo isn't just renewable; it's also incredibly durable.

- Reclaimed Wood: Sourcing wood from old buildings or fallen trees not only gives your space unique character, but it also saves these materials from the landfill.

- Cork: An excellent insulator, it's hypoallergenic and resistant to mold and mildew. It can be used for flooring or wall coverings.

- Eco-Concrete: This variant uses recycled materials as part of its composition, reducing carbon emission during its production.

- Recycled Metal: This uses less energy to manufacture compared to new metal and can give a modern, industrial feel to a design.

10.3. Incorporate Energy-Efficient Features

In a sustainable home, efficiency is key. From energy-saving appliances to lighting options, there's a slew of measures you can take to reduce your home's energy usage.

- Lighting: Replace traditional bulbs with LED or compact fluorescent bulbs. These can use up to 80 percent less energy than conventional bulbs and are generally longer-lasting.

- Appliances: Select appliances with high Energy Star ratings. They consume less electricity and water, which reduces your utility bills and environmental impact simultaneously.

- Solar panels: An excellent renewable source of energy, solar panels can generate electricity for your home, decreasing your dependence on fossil fuels.

- Insulation: Wall, roof, and floor insulations retain heat during the winter and keep your home cool during the summer.

10.4. Embrace Biophilic Design

Biophilic design is about bringing elements of the natural world into your home to promote a sense of well-being. The idea is to recreate the feeling of being in a natural environment, improving your mood and reducing stress.

- Houseplants: They purify the air by absorbing toxins and releasing oxygen. Use plants like succulents, snake plants, or rubber trees that are indoor-hardy and easy to care for.

- Natural Light: Maximize natural light in your space. Make use of skylights, large windows, and glass doors.

- Natural Materials: Use accents with stones, crystals, and wood for a touch of nature.

- Water Features: An indoor water feature such as a small well or fountain can promote serenity and relaxation.

10.5. Reuse, Reduce, Recycle

There is so much you can do by following these three cardinal rules of sustainability.

- Reuse: Opt for upcycling. Be creative and give old items a new lease of life before deciding to throw them away. Antique pieces or hand-me-downs can add vintage charm to your home.

- Reduce: Practice minimalism. Less stuff means less waste. Choose functional and timeless pieces over trendy items that you might tire of quickly.

- Recycle: Buy products made from recycled materials whenever available.

In conclusion, sustainable interior design is about creating a balance between form and function while keeping the environmental impact at the forefront. By implementing the strategies discussed here, you can establish a visually appealing, eco-friendly space that is not only good for you but also beneficial for the planet. Remember, even small changes collectively can account for substantial benefits to the environment.

Chapter 11. Finishing Touches: Accessories and Decorative Elements

Accessories and decorative elements possess vast potential; they can transform mundane spaces into personal reflections of your style and taste. Nevertheless, incorporating them successfully requires strategic planning, careful consideration, and a keen eye for detail.

11.1. Selecting Appropriate Accents

When selecting decorative elements, keep in mind not only the style, color, and texture, but also the scale and proportion. Jewelry for your home, accessories should complement rather than overpowering. Nevertheless, feel free to mix it up — combining a variety of different shapes, sizes, and styles can contribute to a more visually interesting space.

Remember that "less is more." It's often more impactful to have one or two larger pieces than a gathering of smaller knickknacks which can appear cluttered. Let your chosen pieces standout and tell their respective stories.

11.2. Harness the Power of Colors

The use of color can influence the atmosphere within a room, enhancing its overall ambiance. Selecting accessories in accent colors that contrast but coordinate with your dominant color scheme can deliver a vibrant, well-aligned aesthetic that draws the eye. Don't shy away from bolder colors, they can offer a surprising pop of energy which invigorates a space.

Blues and greens suggest a calming environment; reds and oranges, vibrant energy; while neutral tones promote warmth and comfort. It's all about invoking the right emotions in the right spaces.

11.3. Don't Ignore Textures and Patterns

Textures and patterns add a dimension to your aesthetic that simple colours cannot. Even a monotonous room can be positively transformed through the inclusion of such elements.

From fluffy rugs and knitted throws to sleek vases and polished stone, various textures offer a tactile richness that evokes a homely, lived-in feeling. Patterns, also, can introduce rhythm into a room and focus attention, either subtly or assertively, depending in their nature.

11.4. Layering Lighting

Good lighting is about more than seeing clearly; it's about creating an atmosphere.

Incorporate a variety of lighting options within your space to accommodate varying moods and activities. Ambient lighting provides a space its general light level. Task lighting, such as reading lamps, supports specific activities or work spaces. Accent lighting highlights specific areas or items, intensifying the impact of your decorative elements and focal points.

11.5. Style with Personal Items

Personal items such as photos, souvenirs, and collections can help to characterize your style and create a feeling of comfort and familiarity. Display these treasures with pride but don't forget the power of restraint. Remember that negative space can also be a powerful tool.

11.6. Incorporation of Greenery

Greenery brings nature indoors and imparts life to your spaces. Be it a regular-sized potted plant, an indoor tree, or a collection of succulents on a window sill; they all contribute to an environment of freshness and tranquility. Not to mention subtly enhancing air quality!

It's important to consider the care needs of your chosen plants. Do you have the right environment for them to thrive? Drafty windows, or a rarely sun-kissed corner can unfortunately be an inhospitable home for some species.

11.7. Wall Decor

Wall art, mirrors and decorative shelves have the potential to become stunning focal points, drawing the eye and potentially making a space feel larger. However, hanging them correctly is key. Typically, wall decor is hung so that the midpoint is between 57-60 inches from the floor, aligning with the visual horizon of an average person.

Also, consider grouping smaller pieces to create a larger impact. Like a well-curated gallery wall, for example. Experiment with different configurations before making any holes.

11.8. Finishing Touches with Soft Furnishings

Soft furnishings offer impactful yet interchangeable decorations. Cushions, throws, rugs, curtains all fall into this category. They deliver a luxe feeling to seating and surfaces, can tie different elements of your space together, and allow for seasonal décor changes to celebrate holidays or simply refresh a space.

Consider comfort, maintenance, and durability when selecting soft furnishings. They often interact quite intimately with our lives, therefore it's important they fit into your lifestyle as well as your aesthetic.

Understanding the transformative power of accessories and decorative elements will ensure that your living space becomes more than just a house; it becomes a reflection of you: your style, your personality, and your life. With these tips at your disposal, the prospect of decorating your own space will not only be accessible but also an exciting endeavor. Enjoy the journey, and let these finishing touches sign off your dreamy dwelling beautifully!

www.ingramcontent.com/pod-product-compliance
Lightning Source LLC
Chambersburg PA
CBHW071002250726
48663CB00002B/342